My Little One Speaks

TONJA ANDERSON GREENE

Because There's More Publishing | Georgia

Copyright © 2023 by Tonja Anderson Greene

All rights reserved. This book is protected under the copyright laws of the United States of America. This book or any portion thereof may not be reproduced or used in any manner whatsoever without the express written permission of the publisher except for the use of brief quotations in a book review. For permission requests, contact the publisher at the website address below.

ISBN: 979-8-9921977-4-7 (Paperback)
ISBN: 979-8-9921977-5-4 (Hardcover)

Library of Congress Control Number: 2023924251

Printed in the United States of America.

Published by:
Because There's More Publishing LLC
PO Box 390163
Snellville, GA 30039
becausetheresmorepublishing.com

Reviews

This book is easy to read and a source of encouragement for those journeying toward inner healing. Through Tonja's inspiring journey, readers gain valuable insights into identifying the origins of trauma, unveiling its subtle impacts, and comprehending its role in mental health challenges. Yet, beyond mere understanding, Tonja's story instills hope in others navigating their healing journey – showing that overcoming childhood trauma and experiencing profound healing is indeed possible for all. – Chawanda Walker

---

Firstly, I would like to extend my congratulations to the author, Tonja A. Greene, on a job well done. I love everything about this book and highly recommend it to anyone who may be feeling stuck in their healing journey or having trouble starting the healing process. I admire the author's courage and transparency in sharing her life journey and her path to healing with the reader.

Through the author's candid exploration of her fears, honesty, and realization of triggers, readers are given the opportunity to step into her shoes and connect with her on *a deeper, personal level. This book allows readers to unlock, identify, and address those hidden issues that may have kept them captive and in bondage for years. "My Little One Speaks," in my opinion, is a must read.*

I particularly loved the "Reflection" section after each chapter, which encourages readers to reflect, discover, and begin their own healing process. The book is very easy to read and profoundly impactful. Readers will undoubtedly find the exploration of self-discovery and self-awareness, as well as the introspection encouraged by the author, to be the starting point of their healing journey.

Reader, I strongly encourage and admonish you to allow this book to minister to and speak to the inner child within you. – Bridget G.

Foreword

Being afforded the opportunity to write the foreword for Ms. Tonja Anderson-Greene's book is an absolute honor. I do not accept this honor lightly; I am humbled and moved by the gesture, as well as by this body of work. As a leader in the Kingdom and in the marketplace, I have met a lot of people and have had an opportunity to get to know some of them more intimately than others. Some have shared stories of great support and tremendous upbringings, while others' stories are quite different. And then, others' stories are desolate, if not downright heart-wrenching.

Although I have known Tonja for quite some time and am familiar with her story, it is through the request to write this foreword that has offered me the opportunity to acknowledge and establish another level of respectful appreciation for the awesomeness of this woman of God.

This book speaks to Tonja's journey as a silent warrior who found her voice… and in the process, located her wings to soar!

Many go through life not knowing who they are or without timely, life teachers who assist in showing them the way to find their identity and help to cultivate the strength in knowing it. Without knowing who you are (or whose you are!), challenges that will be faced in life have a far greater impact on how you may see yourself, as well as how you would choose to navigate situations. In this body of work, Tonja shares the life struggles that she endured. She also gives an account of the journey experienced in finding God and developing a relationship with Him. Once she yielded her trust to Him, this then led to the direction in which she began to do the self-work necessary to trade paths with her past and began to travel on the road to becoming the person that she is today.

This book is a life-story representation of **Beauty for Ashes**, that hopefully will inspire others to seek and discover a closer relationship with God, do their own self-work, as well as the self-discovery needed to trade paths with their own pasts, and then, themselves, identify the road to their freedom and divine purpose.

Lady Jameia Johnson
Rhema Wind Ministries
Morrow, Georgia

Contents

Introduction	9
Chapter 1: Journey	12
Chapter 2: The Unveiling	23
Chapter 3: Honesty	36
Chapter 4: Fear	49
Chapter 5: Trust	60
Chapter 6: Healing	68
Quick Scripture Reference Guide	79
Daily Affirmations	83
Helpful Resources	88
About the Author	91

Introduction

My Little One Speaks is a short story about my journey to rediscovering and healing the child within. As a nurse, I've spent decades tending to the wounds of others and helping them in their healing journey. But under that smile lay wounds deeply buried in my subconscious mind. However, what was buried was slowly resurrecting and making its appearance in my adult life - so much so that it threatened to sideline my present. I found myself at a fork in the road; I had to make a decision.

[1]It is reported that one in three girls and one in five boys have experienced sexual abuse before the age of eighteen years old. [2]Unfortunately, 30% of sexual abuse cases are never reported. Many survivors choose not to report these experiences

---

[1] The Advocacy Center. https://www.theadvocacycenter.org
[2] The Advocacy Center. https://www.theadvocacycenter.org

due to feelings of shame and assumed blame or fault, which can cause them to suffer in silence. Moreover, sexual abuse has no biases. It happens across all races, ethnic groups, cultures, and socioeconomic and education levels.

I was one of those who did not speak out. It was my little secret; one I planned to take to my grave. But I was triggered, and the place I thought I had moved far away from came flooding back - I was that vulnerable little girl again. In that moment, I had to make a choice: to confront the pain and be healed or remain silent and hope no one else triggers the little one within.

Before you proceed to the next chapter, let me forewarn you. This book contains sensitive content that may trigger some individuals. My story is filled with highs and lows, as well as transparent reflections.

If you find yourself in the pages of this book, I pray you take courage and embark on your own journey of healing. I pray that the sharing of my story fills your heart with hope and a knowing from God that healing, restoration, and freedom from past trauma are possible.

Chapter 1

Journey
An Awkward Beginning

Several years ago, I discovered journaling. The process of writing my thoughts on paper, never wanting to forget my life's journey was freeing. Through the good, the bad, and the ugly, writing became a source of healing, security, direction, identification, and confirmation. At the same time, it gave me a voice. It opened doors that were locked. It closed doors that brought pain. It led me to secret places with God. It also gave me a chance to be me. Writing provided me with privacy and honesty; it was a judgment-free zone.

I was about twenty years old when life's doors began to open for me. I attended a youth service with one of my sisters. The concert was outside in an open field. There were hundreds of young people, both black and white, singing, clapping, lifting their hands, praising, and worshipping God together. The music was not really the type of music I was accustomed to; this was new. I had never experienced anything like this before. It was amazing and overwhelming all in the same breath. After the church service, I was asked about salvation several times. Very cute and calm, I replied, "I'm okay thank you." I continued to smile, thinking to myself "I am ready to go!"

Please note that I had been attending church my entire life and had said the sinners' prayer some years ago. Thus, I had my fire insurance and believed I was good. However, I knew there was more God wanted me to experience in Him.

Fast forward several years, and I returned to that same church where I attended that outdoor concert and became a member. I also served as one of their youth leaders. Nonetheless, I was full of anger and shame, which caused me to mistreat my sister. I would call her ugly names and say very mean, nasty, and negative things to her and about her. One day while attending church, I heard of a ministry called *Overcomers*. It was a prerequisite to the *ACOA (Adult Children of Alcoholics)* ministry. Sadly, we came from a generation of alcoholics. Both of our parents consumed alcohol. So my sister and I decided to join this ministry. I was very optimistic about it. It was my desire to become more aware of my behavior and change some things about myself.

Several weeks had passed and the class was coming to an end. I thought to myself, "This wasn't so bad." However, there was a price increase, so we decided to stop. This was a blessing in disguise, as it caused me to pivot and focus my attention on weight loss, which inadvertently lead me to the place where I am today.

At this time, I was about thirty pounds overweight. I tried fad diets and pills but to no avail. One principal topic of discussion in the class I attended was on addictive behaviors and how a person responds to those behaviors. First, [3]addictive behaviors are strong desires or compulsions that cause you to engage in activity or behavior despite the negative impact it has on the individual. Overeating, gambling, drinking, promiscuity, and shopping can all become or are in some people addictive behaviors. For me, being overweight provided security. According to the Baptist Health article, [4]*Psychological Effects of Obesity,* some people are overweight or diagnosed as obese due to emotional eating because they fall short of dealing with the issues of life. Later, I discovered

---

[3] 10 Patterns of Addictive Behavior | Psychology Today.
https://www.psychologytoday.com/us/blog/science-choice/201702/10-patterns-addictive-behavior
[4] Psychological Effects Of Obesity
https://www.baptisthealth.com/blog/family-health/psychological-effects-of-obesity

this was me! My next step was OA or Overeaters Anonymous, since dieting was not working. I had two main reasons for joining this class: it was free, and I needed to lose weight.

"I'M HERE!" was my initial thought, followed by "Sign me up!" Unbeknownst to me, this was a twelve-step program, and it would change my life forever. My transformation started with the first meeting. I told myself, "You can do this. You are tough. Don't be emotional and cry. Just do enough to blend in. You are not like these other ladies. Girl, you know your goals and purpose for this class. It is to lose weight and get your sexy back, and THAT'S IT! Now, let's see if this works. If not, just move on. Nothing can happen if you don't try." Yes, I had this whole conversation with myself; remember, this is a judgment-free zone.

Each week, I would get on the scale before class to show I lost weight. I thought to myself, "Oh yes, I got this in the bag, and I didn't even have to participate that much!" However, my little inner celebration came to a screeching halt when one of the group leaders began to invade my privacy and intrude into my world during a round-robin discussion. My first thoughts were of anger. "Why does she want to know what's going on with me? I'm losing weight weekly; life is great" - or so I thought.

Although thoughts were raging in my head, I was not one to express my feelings. I was a passive, non-confrontational person at this time. However, the group leader very compassionately asked me to do an assignment and to be completely honest with myself. I agreed to do the assignment, though I secretly had a slight attitude. She disrupted my groove. It wasn't my intention to put much effort into this program.

I remember going home to get my notebook to start the assignment, but I only did enough so that I could return to class. The following week, feeling okay that I had at least written down something, I stood up and proceeded with my story. Upon completion, the group leader looked at me with a smirk on her face. She politely stated, "Thank you for sharing, but you are not being honest. You are wearing a mask. You are in denial." My eyes grew large in amazement, but my thoughts toward her were not good. "How dare she say this to me? She doesn't know me!" A few moments later, she asked if I was okay. I lied and said yes. She started to venture further. She asked me if I would trust her and submit to an exercise. With much hesitation, but ensuring that I stayed in full control of my emotions, I said yes. Then, the floodgates opened. Somewhere in the midst of me closing my eyes and answering some of the questions, I started to cry. She embraced me and told me to go home and continue with the assignment.

I do not remember if it was during the questions or shortly after that I recalled being inappropriately touched at the age of thirteen or fourteen. I did not know what to do or how to feel about this discovery. Honestly, I felt numb, lost, shocked, ashamed, in disbelief, and angry all at once. Thoughts began to flood my mind. "Who can I tell? What will they think? Will they believe me? I can't tell anyone. They will think it was my fault or that I desired it."

Now at home, I sat with tears streaming down my face. All I could do was cry. I wanted to reach out to my family, but at the same time, I didn't want to alarm anyone. This was the beginning of sleepless nights and several million thoughts parading around in my mind. The next class couldn't come fast enough. It was one of the longest weeks of my life.

Class time finally arrived, and I looked forward to going for several reasons: I felt relieved, I survived, and I was told I was not alone. A big smile appeared on my face amidst the tears. Hugs, words of comfort, and encouragement were just what I needed, and that is just what I received.

As time progressed and engagement within the group increased, the authenticity allowed me to let down my defenses. Many of the ladies would use the term "my little girl" when they talked about certain situations. I would say to myself, "Now they have really gone crazy. What in the world have I gotten myself into? Wow, these ladies are speaking in third person now!" I was taken aback, and I'm sure my thoughts were on display with my facial expressions. I have been told by various people that my face speaks volumes. Feeling lost in the moment, I didn't know what to do until my neighbor whispered to me, "You have a little girl too." At that time, I was single with no children, so naturally, my response to her was, "No, I do not have any children." Needless to say, searching for my little girl became my assignment.

> "Your inner child is not a "childlike personality." Rather, it's the part of your subconscious mind that experienced and still remembers your childhood moments and emotions, both good and bad."
>
> Psych Central

Reflection:

Stepping into the unknown and sharing your truth can be intimidating, even downright awkward at times. Have you experienced any of these moments? If so, what motivated you to push through and continue the journey?

Chapter 2

The Unveiling:
Connecting with My Inner Child

"What a journey, and it is just the beginning. But I can do this." The assignment was all about self-discovery and self-awareness, and it entailed the following:

- spending time with myself
- asking questions
- revisiting childhood memories
- visualizing myself as a child
- acknowledgment of my inner child
- journaling my thoughts, emotions, and reactions
- writing and speaking affirmations
- practicing self-compassion and self-love

"I know me. This should be pretty easy…shouldn't it be?" I said to myself. It turned out to be one of the hardest things I've done.

So, I started this assignment by asking my mother and siblings about my childhood. I looked through numerous photo albums and one particular photo stood out to me. I have beautiful brown skin, all of my fingers and toes, sandy brown hair in three pigtails with white bows, beautiful big brown eyes, a nose, and a smile. Her name was Tonja and she looked like me. I recognized the photo, but did not know why that photo specifically struck me. Uncertain about what the rest of my story entailed, I felt like these inquiries for my family would help me to uncover the full story.

I returned to class feeling accomplished. I had written down all the features of the little girl and thought I was on the right track. When asked, did I complete my assignment, with full confidence and a smile, I said, "Yes!" I began to read what I had written and to my disappointment my class was not impressed at all. When I finished speaking someone asked, "How much time did you spend on your project?" I responded, "About fifteen to thirty minutes." I was being truthful. I had only spent, at the most, about thirty minutes on this assignment. Another voice responded, "I really would like for you to experience a breakthrough in this area. Will you consider revisiting this assignment?" Feeling slightly inadequate, with hesitation, I answered, "Sure, I will try."

Riding home after class, feeling puzzled, I asked myself, "What does she want from me?"

A few days passed and it was the night before class again. I thought about what I needed to do to revisit the assignment. I did not want to lie in class. Even if I lied, they would hold me accountable and more than likely dig even further. "Maybe I should just quit. She did make me look stupid during the last class," I thought to myself. "What else is there for me to discover about the little girl within?"

An honest introspection: I am a great starter, but even better at not finishing. If there are things in my life that cause me any level of discomfort, stress, pressure, or slightly push me out of my comfort zone, I will stop. It is much easier to make an excuse and justify my reasoning for not completing or finishing whatever it is that I started. Interestingly enough, I have a best friend, and her name is Procrastination. She makes suggestions to me, prompting me to think if I wait long enough then I won't have to do something. Sometimes, she just lets me be flat-out lazy. "I'll do it later" is my favorite response. However, I desire to be a better me. Challenging myself to heal is the best gift I can give myself.

For those of you who have never attended a support group or 12-step program, let me give you a little visual. It is a small or large group of committed people with similar concerns or experiences who meet regularly to provide support, encouragement and share information with each other. Some groups are open, others are closed due to the nature of the issues discussed. My group was small and closed. It was very intimate. With the outpour of love that I received from my group, it encouraged me to hang in there.

"Who is Tonja?" I asked myself this question as I stood in the mirror staring at myself. Five, ten, fifteen minutes passed with no answer. Whew, that had to be the longest fifteen minutes of my life. As I walked away from the mirror I whispered, "I did it!" Now, I won't have to lie in class tomorrow."

Several weeks had gone by and still nothing. I remember feeling frustrated and afraid. I would repeatedly say to myself "I love you," and I would hug myself. I remembered my classmates telling me to stay consistent, that it would happen. Nothing. I didn't see my little one within.

More time passed. My feelings ran rapidly during this time. I started to feel anxious, strange, and awkward all at the same time. I started to question, "Does this really work or am I just making a fool out of myself? I am an adult. How can I speak to a child inside of me?"

I continued to stare at myself in the mirror. I was so quiet you could hear a needle drop. Without warning, I began to cry – no, not cry, but sob. Tears streaming down my face with frustration I screamed, "THIS IS NOT WORKING FOR ME! WHAT AM I DOING WRONG?!" I started hugging myself and saying, "I love me!" I was doing everything that I was told to do. Feeling frustrated, angry, and scared, I reached for my paper, pen, and began to write. I started to write everything that had just taken place.

DID YOU KNOW?

We hold any or all childhood trauma, thoughts, pain, and reactions in our unconscious minds. It is a place where it is often forgotten, and it remains hidden until it is triggered.

So, what are emotional triggers? According to the Ridgeview Behavioral Hospital's article, [5]*How To Identify Emotional Triggers in 3 Steps,* emotional triggers are thoughts, words, memories, objects, or people that spark intense negative emotions. Sometimes, we respond to triggers with facial or body expressions or even outbursts. Have you ever heard someone say, "Where did that (reaction) come from?" A trigger can cause that kind of reaction.

> [6]*"Hiding pain doesn't heal it. Instead, it often surfaces in your adult life, showing up as distress in personal relationships or difficulty meeting your own needs. Working to heal your inner child can help you address some of these issues."*
> Crystal Raypole

I want to make a note that meeting my little one took some time; I did not meet her in just one sitting. It took several months before I could

---

[5] How to Identify Emotional Triggers In 3 Steps | Ridgeview Hospital. https://ridgeviewhospital.net/how-to-identify-emotional-triggers-in-3-steps/

[6] 8 Ways to Start Healing Your Inner Child | Healthline. Crystal Raypole. https://www.healthline.com/health/mental-health/inner-child-healing

visualize her in my mind. One day, in my quest to discover my little girl, I closed my eyes and I saw a small silhouette of a little girl hiding behind a wall. I only saw her for a few seconds. She did not speak any words; she just peeked through.

I was excited but still uneasy because I did not know what to do next. I quickly opened my eyes and looked around the room, reminding myself that it was only me in the room. I sat quietly for a moment and thought to myself, "Wow, what just happened? Did this just take place?" With my pen and paper, I started to write. With tears of joy in my eyes, I wrote down my accomplishment in finally seeing my little girl, but this was just the beginning.

---

[7] "Healing your inner child can be a powerful process that may help you resolve past traumas and emotional wounds...That said, it often takes time, patience, and resilience, which is just one reason

---

[7] Healing your inner child: Tips and techniques. BetterHelp Editorial Team. https://www.betterhelp.com/advice/parenting/healing-your-inner-child-tips-and-techniques/

many choose to work through the process with the help of a mental health professional." - BetterHelp

For the next leg of my journey, I was told to build a relationship with my little girl. This was where the work began. I took joy in just seeing her in my mind. "How could I move forward to seeing more of her?" was the question.

One day I sat down and closed my eyes, and my little girl appeared again. When I saw her, I began to love and affirm her. I looked at her. I saw her beautiful brown skin, her sandy brown hair, and her big brown eyes. Those eyes held so much sadness and no smile. She had nothing to say or verbally express. I quickly opened my eyes and began to write.

I wrote about the grief I felt and sustained. This interaction went on for a long period. I did not want to rush anything. Embracing everything is vital to our relationship. There are no time limits when you are investing in yourself. Time continued to pass and there was no growth from what I could measure in our relationship. I began to wonder why my little girl hadn't spoken to me yet. I thought I made her feel welcomed and loved, but this relationship was still new, and I was learning about her.

I remember one particular time so vividly when my little girl spoke to me. It was just an introduction, but words, nonetheless. As I saw her face in my mind overwhelmed with sadness, I began to cry. I tried to interpret what her eyes wanted to express to me - hurt, pain, loneliness, and abandonment - all of which I could relate to. I pulled myself away for a moment and began to write about my emotions.

I closed my eyes again and when I saw her, I immediately apologized to her. I assured her that she was not at fault. I told her that she was not a bad little girl and that she did not do anything to cause those transgressions against her. I promised her that she would never be abandoned again. A short time after my apologizing I heard a small whisper, "Hi." I quickly looked around in amazement. I heard the whisper again, "Hi, my name is Tonja." Wow, a miracle had just taken place. I just spoke to my little girl. She continued, "I am the little girl that lives inside of you. I have your heart, your eyes, everything the same as you. When you looked in the mirror you didn't see me because you didn't know you. Not until you were ready and willing to know me, did I allow you to connect with me." This may sound strange, but I started to be free from bondage after this interaction. It was the beginning of my making peace with the past, so I could move forward.

Reflection:

When was the last time you dedicated time to (re)discover and get to know you? What new things did you learn about yourself? How did your journey of self-discovery help you to become a better person?

_____

_____

_____

_____

_____

_____

_____

_____

_____

_____

_____

_____

_____

_____

Chapter 3

Honesty
Sharing My Truth

The past is the place of reference that I use to encourage my present and propel me to my future. God never intended for us to get stuck there. It's not only okay, but necessary for us to move forward. Having said that, this voyage can be full of peaks and valleys.

There are hundreds of publications throughout the world that provide direction on self-help and inner healing. Whatever route you choose to take, my recommendation is that you find a therapist and stay committed to the process to achieve the desired result – healing. Ecclesiastes 9:11 informs us that the race is not given to the swift nor the battle to the strong, but to the person that endures to the end. Endurance builds strength, power, hope, and self-awareness. The moral example of the scripture would be the story of the Tortoise and the Hare.

The Need for Honesty

If asked, "Are you honest?", the majority of people would say yes and give examples to prove how honest they are. However, honesty is a lifestyle. Self-honesty is an area where some may waver. This is an area where I had to do some self-examining. On my road to healing, I had to remove many of my masks and come face to face with my issues and emotions. That was extremely hard for me.

My house felt empty at times while growing up. We had fun playing games, laughing at each other. Yet there was no real bond between my siblings and me. We loved and cared for each other, but something was missing. Some people would call our upbringing dysfunctional; we lived in survival mode. Our parents did the best they could with the tools they were given.

I am the baby of the family. The fifth girl and tenth child, I had no voice. I was always told to, "Shut up!" or "Your opinion doesn't matter." Everyone spoke over me and spoke for me. As a result of this treatment, my communication with others was negatively affected. As mentioned before, I was very passive. As a child and teen, kids picked on me and called me ugly names. As a result, I developed low self-esteem. Growing up, young boys touched my buttocks inappropriately and said inappropriate things about the shape of my body. Their actions made me angry, and their touch made me feel so uncomfortable. I felt like an outcast.

> "Feeling like you must behave in a way that is inauthentic to your true self is exhausting, especially when you believe that others will not accept you or punish you for showing your true self."
>
> Dr. Amy Marschall

My desperation for friends led to my becoming a people pleaser. Even the people who I thought were my friends made fun of me. Wanting to experience some sense of true friendship, I ignored the behavior. I would go the extra mile for others and deny myself, only to receive disappointment and rejection in return. Broken promises and trust became normal. I must admit that I am all too familiar with betrayal. It showed up in different forms: gossip, abandonment, disloyalty, deception, and breach of trust, just to name a few. I dwelt in pain, hurt, and disappointment. I had to learn how to discern who to trust; trustworthy people are hard to find.

The Realization

Many seasons would pass, and I was still writing in my journal weekly. By now, I was married for a few years and life was good, so I thought.

In conversations with my husband, I started to become triggered. I finally revealed to him my past trauma as a teenager. He was perplexed and speechless. He began to comfort me. He also expressed some anger and frustration because the trauma was caused by someone my family trusted. Soon after I told my husband of my trauma, I shared the news with two of my sisters. They both cried and apologized for not being there to protect me. I assured them that it wasn't their fault. I expressed with much confidence that I would no longer be a victim of shame.

No longer able to deal with the anger and triggers, I began to have tantrums in my marriage. I threw tantrums when things did not go my way. Unable to verbalize my needs or concerns, I would throw dishes against the wall. Yet, I felt like the broken dishes on the floor. Surprisingly, breaking the dishes was a form of release for me. I've always considered myself to be a good Christian young lady, and I did not want to destroy that image. However, when I argued with my husband someone else came out. Someone I didn't even recognize. I would curse my husband out, say ugly things to him, making sure to hit him below the belt. I would act out as well. The "Victim Mentality" was in full effect. There was a time when I jumped on top of a moving car while my husband was driving it. I wasn't even worried about my safety or who saw me on top of the car. Now let's pause for a second. Yes, a trigger can have you so far out there that you will do some of the wildest things. Please do not be like me at that moment. I was so full of anger and rage, but it only showed up at home.

Nevertheless, I continued to attend church, paid my tithes and offering, and participated in various ministries. You know the good Christian. I had so much going on in my life, but no one took the time to inquire. But if I'm honest, if someone did inquire, I'm sure I would've told them that I was okay. My attitude was that people should stay in their own lanes and if you crossed into mine, I was going to let you have it.

I became defensive and outspoken. The passive Tonja was non-existent. I knew how to wear my masks well. Drinking wine and alcohol eventually drifted into my life. My drinking started off as social, then progressed into hiding and ultimately routine. I was becoming someone who I said I would never become, an alcoholic like my dad. He displayed such negative behavior and said such damaging words while drinking. He was one man on Sunday through Thursday and on the other days a different person, like Dr. Jekyll and Mr. Hyde. I was becoming him and fast.

I no longer wanted the consistent back and forth in my marriage. Your home should be a place of peace. Challenges happen, but it is how you handle them that makes the difference. Marriage is not for children; it is for mature adults, and it requires teamwork. My husband and I hit one of those rough patches, and I returned to therapy fully uninhibited this time around. With confidence, I walked through the therapist's doors thinking to myself, my secrets were out. I had no more skeletons in my closet.

After attending several sessions, my past was discussed, and the therapist began investigating my childhood. My answers did not correspond with her knowledge. More exercises were introduced and that is when I discovered that my first encounter with molestation was at the age of five or six years old, not thirteen or fourteen like I previously remembered. I was devastated. I cried and I cried. The feelings of shame returned like never before. I returned home after that session unsure of what to do or think. I reached home and entered my room, and I cried some more. Thank God my husband and child were not home. I didn't want to have to explain what was wrong with me.

I recalled my mother punishing and whooping me for doing something I was told to do by someone else. In our home, teaching and conversations were replaced with confusion and fear. Many times, I did not know what it was I did wrong. I had so many emotions for a small child and those emotions were exploding in my adult life.

Now, I realized why my little girl was not a teen, when we met, the trauma started earlier. Everything was out on the table. No more secrets.

No more hidden trauma. Now, I could complete my healing journey.

Sharing My Truth

My husband has seen the good, the bad, and the ugly. On many occasions we had conversations about life and family. I finally shared my latest revelation with him. He was shocked. He didn't immediately respond. He just walked away. After a short time, he returned to the room with tears flowing down his face and we embraced. No words were spoken, we just embraced each other. In a soft voice, he uttered, "I'm sorry and I love you so much." My inner thoughts said, he was probably thinking this woman got a lot going on. As usual, negative thoughts rushed to my mind. I'm thinking, where do I go from here?

The uncovering of earlier trauma finally explained the why to some of the triggers I felt. The relationship with my sisters had been repaired by now and I sensed I needed to be honest with them as well. I felt like a broken jar repaired with glue that may leak at any given moment, if water, heat, or pressure were to be applied. Lord help me!

Honesty is a component of maturity. Being honest with yourself may feel a little awkward and may appear difficult at first, but as you continue to put it into practice, your outcome will be great. I had to be honest with God and myself and ask Him the question, "Why did you allow these tragedies to take place in my life?" His answer was, "I didn't allow it. The devil by way of those people with some mental dysfunction violated you." With tears in my eyes, anger, and pain in my heart, I screamed. I didn't understand.

Before I proceed further, let me offer this piece of advice for others embarking on their own healing journey. Be careful to whom you share your story. You would not meet a stranger and tell them all your deepest, darkest secrets. Prayerfully, the person you choose to reveal those things to is a professional therapist or a person with whom you have built a sense of security and trust. For example, I would not tell a person that I have been dating for a short period of time about my life's trauma. If you are seriously dating, engaged, or married, you owe it to that person to be true and allow them to decide if they want to continue with the relationship once you've disclosed those secrets.

Again, hidden triggers will show themselves in your relationship. If your significant other chooses to stay, there is an opportunity for both of you to grow and strengthen your relationship. If the relationship ends after secrets are revealed, know that you can heal and move forward with your life. Furthermore, it is possible for you to experience a healthy and fulfilling relationship. Being honest with yourself and others is powerful!

Reflection:

How honest are you with yourself and with others? Have you ever felt the need to mask or hide your true self for acceptance? How did you overcome the need to be a people pleaser and embrace you?

_____
_____
_____
_____
_____
_____
_____
_____
_____
_____
_____
_____

Chapter 4

Fear
God Help Me!

Anger, rage, tantrums, wanting to be heard, wanting attention, wanting to share, being afraid, unable to communicate my needs, frustration, and fear are all the emotions and feelings I experienced, and sometimes simultaneously. However, the greatest emotional hindrance for me was fear.

My introduction to fear was at the tender age of five. I remember one particular Saturday night, climbing out of a two-story apartment building window, sliding down a pole, and running down the sidewalk. My father had been drinking and my parents were arguing like they did every weekend. However, this time I heard a very loud noise that scared me. So I ran, jumped on the bed, pushed out the window screen, and out the window I went. My sister later found me crying and brought me back home. I did not want to go back into the house. I was still crying, but she assured me that I would be okay. Despite her reassurance, I was still afraid.

The Oxford English Dictionary defines fear as *an unpleasant feeling or emotion caused by the belief that someone or something is dangerous or likely to cause pain or threat.* Although fear is a natural emotion that can help us to stay safe in dangerous situations, excessive fear can be problematic and even paralyzing. Fear can be triggered by a number of factors, such as a dog bite, past trauma or abuse, scary movie, lack of information (unknown), environmental dangers, and more, whether real or imagined. Some fears are more easily adaptable than others. Therefore, not everyone reacts to fear in the same manner. Some may react with racing heartbeats and increased adrenaline, while others experience shortness of breath, muscle tension, sweating, and even confusion and anxiety, just to name a few.

Unfortunately, there was a time in my life when fear consumed me. My mind raced with foreboding thoughts and feelings that something bad was going to happen. I was afraid of people, sounds, and going places. I was truly in bondage. I was a prisoner in my home and my mind. Fear hurts. It destroys and pushes you into isolation. I would cry and weep, but I was afraid to tell a soul. I was embarrassed and humiliated. I was even afraid to drive anywhere besides work and even that became a struggle.

I do not recall how or when it started, but I remember leaving for work one day; it was around five p.m. on a Friday evening. While driving on the expressway, I hit a bump in the road. I got off the expressway to take the side streets, then got back on the expressway, then back to the side streets. This went on for several hours! I started to cry and experienced a panic attack. I was afraid to answer my cellphone, my mind was all over the place. I remember my husband calling me and I finally got the courage to answer. By this time, it was about ten at night. He said, "Are you okay? Just come on, I will meet you off the interstate." We met up, and he followed me home.

Once we arrived home, I started to cry all over again. I was scared and felt overwhelmed. My head was hurting as I tried to replay what had just taken place. I got no rest that night, I was full of anxiety. That wasn't the only incident I had while driving, but that was the incident that pushed my family to the edge.

"You are going to see someone," my husband requested. "Please understand, I do not think you are crazy, but that is not normal behavior," he stated.

My initial thoughts were, "I am a professional. What do I look like?" My pride started to rise and soon after, shame came in and I became very emotional. "What will people say or think? God, why me? I have experienced so much - why this? What is this anyway?" I was angry all over again. Angrily, I agreed to go see a doctor. Thank God I did.

I was diagnosed with anxiety and OCD (Obsessive Compulsive Disorder) Checker. A checker is a person who constantly checks on things to prevent catastrophes. I was prescribed medication, which I took faithfully, and started attending therapy again.

Fear will keep you from living a fulfilling life and realizing your God-given purpose. You don't have to be consumed with fear, nor do you have to be overtaken by its attachments, such as depression, excessive sleeping, overeating, drinking alcohol, or recreational and prescription drug use. All of this is done to avoid or suppress some negative thought or emotion.

For me, it was insomnia, lack of eating, always second-guessing myself, and thoughts of physical or spiritual suicide. In the beginning, I didn't know how to use the Word of God to conquer my battles. As a result of this, I felt so defeated at times. I wanted to throw in my white towel and forfeit the fight. The more negative things would happen, the more I had to learn to lean on God. My life was a mess! My mind was running non-stop with worry, stress, and anxiety.

I never imagined my mind would venture into some of the dark places that it did. Nightmares of family members dying, sometimes I would even yell out in my sleep only to wake up and realize it was a dream. I desperately desired to rest because I was tired. But sleep eluded me. I would sleep five to fifteen minutes, only to be awakened for hours out of fear of nightmares. I would get angry and frustrated because I was so sleepy. The insomnia had me physically tired and overwhelmed. I longed to be free from negative thoughts and behaviors, but I did not know how to accomplish it. I wanted to share my life's direction with others but didn't want to be judged or ridiculed for expressing my thoughts. I did not want to actually kill myself; I just wanted the pain to stop. GOD HELP ME!

God is joy and peace, not turmoil and hell. I was at the altar weekly for prayer because my thoughts were causing me so much pain. There were times when I wanted to take my head off my shoulders just to release all of the negative thoughts. Once all the thoughts were cleared, I could put my head back on. I had to lean into Isaiah 26:3 NLT and trust God to keep me in perfect peace as I trust and fix my thoughts on Him.

AND HE DID!

God helped me through medicine, therapy, prayer, and His Word. My healing incorporated both the spiritual and clinical. One isn't an antithesis of the other. God can use both to facilitate your healing. It doesn't make God any less God, nor does it make you any less spiritual.

I needed to pause and interject this for my brothers and sisters wrestling with getting professional help.

Also, I listened to the CD, "How to Change Negative Thoughts with Positive Thoughts," while driving in my car. It was my road companion for two years. You do not have to own negative thoughts when they come to your mind. You can reject the thoughts.

2 Timothy 1:7 states, "God has not given me a spirit of fear and intimidation but of power, love, and self-discipline" (NLT).

God is love and His love towards me does not cause torment in my mind. I posted this note to myself all over my house, in my car, at my work computer, and other places. I was determined to live free

The following scriptures were a source of comfort and strength in my journey. They carried me through some of the hardest times in my life. May you find a resting place in God's Word.

Isaiah 41:10 (NIV) *Do not fear for I am with you, do not be dismayed for I am God.*

Psalm 56:3 *When I am afraid, I put my hope in you.*

Philippians 4:6-7 (NIV) *Don't worry about anything instead pray about everything. Tell God what you need and thank him for all he has done. Then you will experience God's peace which exceeds anything we can understand.*

Reflection:

Has fear hindered your progress? Has it prevented you from doing something you knew God called you to do? How did you overcome that fear? If you are still in your healing journey, what steps are you taking to ensure fear does not become your driver?

_____

_____

_____

_____

_____

_____

_____

_____

_____

_____

_____

_____

_____

Chapter 5

Trust

A Journey of Growth

Trust is a five-letter word with a powerful meaning. Merriam-Webster's dictionary defines trust as:

- *assured reliance on the character, ability, strength, or truth of someone or something*
- *to rely on the truthfulness or accuracy of: to believe*

The Bible Counseling Database defines trust as *a firm reliance, assurance and belief on God and His Word.*

I am sure most of you have heard or read Proverbs 3:5, "Trust in the Lord with all your heart and lean not to your own understanding." As a born-again believer, I am a witness that this particular passage is often quoted, but the question for me was how to apply it to my life.

On multiple occasions, I have been told to just trust God. "But, how do you trust God?" was my rebuttal question, which often went unanswered. I know the Bible says to do it, but how? Is there a five-step method? At the end of those five steps, will trust suddenly appear?

Because of my trauma, I wrestled with this question. I knew that I was supposed to trust God. On the other hand, the Word says that man was made in His image, and I had been betrayed by the men in my life. So, how could I trust God? Will, He hurt me too? I had unfairly grouped God in the same category as the people who hurt me, simply because He created them. Having said that, none of my thoughts came as a surprise to God (Psalm 139:1-2). He knew me. Now, it was time for me to get to know Him.

> *God is not human, that he should lie, not a human being, that he should change his mind. Does he speak and then not act? Does he promise and not fulfill?*
> Numbers 23:19

I can recall when trusting God was difficult. I would read my Bible trying to memorize the scriptures and my concept of trust did not change. As a matter of fact, I became angrier because I invested my time and was still left with no understanding, just frustration. There were times I would reach for my journal and begin to examine and extract my life's issues. I had to commit to releasing the old lies, thoughts, habits, and memories to replace them with truth as my perspective on life changed. After some time, I learned to trust my own thoughts, emotions, and decisions. While growing in my relationship with God, I started to trust Him, gain confidence, assurance, and an acknowledgement of self-worth.

I had to tell myself daily that I would not take part in self-sabotage, self-betrayal or become a victim of mistrust.

While writing this chapter, I was reminded of the famous line by William Shakespeare, "To thine own self be true." This popular line has various interpretations, but for me, it reminds me to always examine myself with honesty and truth. This is so important, because one's perception of the truth can vary depending on the lens in which that truth is filtered.

There are times when truth seems so demanding, heavy, and massive, that you question whether or not you can accomplish the task. Other times, the illusion (which consists of lies and deceptions) seems more appealing and glamourous, and if you are not aware, you can find yourself drifting toward the appearance of a false reality, instead of moving towards truth.

I had to own the fact that keeping my vision clear was my responsibility, so I wouldn't embrace illusions. This required me to be honest with myself daily and submit to God's plan for my life.

What voids are you trying to fill? What are you afraid to confess? What are your darkest, closest secrets? Could there be something hidden and deeply rooted within you that you may not be able to identify with at this very moment? Just because you cannot identify "it" does not mean that it does not exist or is not present. Your "it" can be whatever is holding you hostage or whatever you are holding hostage. Until you can acknowledge it, you will not be able to break free from the bondage of it. Freedom means you are no longer in bondage to it, nor a victim of it.

Trusting God teaches us to maintain accountability. It requires us to freely relinquish the reins of control and follow His plan for our lives. I'll be the first to admit that it is not always "cookies and cream". To be quite honest, there will be times when you will feel like God is not there, but He is always there.

There will be times of unanswered prayers, but remember delay does not mean denial (Isaiah 40:31). If we look to others, we may be disappointed and dismayed. Sometimes, we build a false sense of security in things and people when both are subject to change and can fail. The most secure place is in God and investing in that relationship has eternal rewards.

Having said that, trusting God is a personal response to your RELATIONSHIP with Him - our loving Father, ABBA, my beloved Daddy.

Trust is a journey of growth and surrendering to God that advances to submission and obedience. It is not always easy or fair, but success is guaranteed by choosing a perfect God who will never let you down.

Reflection:

How is your trust barometer? Did past trauma affect your ability to trust? How did you move past the hurt and open yourself up to trusting God and those He sent into your life?

_____

_____

_____

_____

_____

_____

_____

_____

_____

_____

_____

_____

_____

Chapter 6

Healing
I'm Here

Upon completing this book, I was unsure of what the end would consist of. However, I wanted to finish with several words of encouragement. Out of all of the scriptures on healing, Matthew 15: 21-28 impacted me the most. The woman in this passage knew if she was persistent enough in her faith, her daughter would be healed. I believe that when we are persistent in seeking God, healing as well as other miracles, signs and wonders can take place.

Merriam-Webster's dictionary defines healing as *to make free from injury or disease : to make sound or whole*. I would personally define healing as the restoration of health and wholeness to one's physical, mental, and spiritual being.

I attended a church conference on healing some years ago. I did everything the pastor asked. I shouted, leaped, turned around, and spoke to my neighbor. I followed all the instructions that were given. However, during the service, I did not feel a change. I thought to myself, "Maybe I will receive my healing in the morning." But when I awoke, there was still no change. Then I thought, "Maybe God will do it on Sunday at the end of the conference." But Sunday came and left - still no change. By Monday morning, I was convinced that no change was going to occur, well at least not during this conference.

Disappointed, I figured that God has His time. All was well with my physical body: maybe God was just doing physical healings during this conference. I always thought that you had to be "super spiritual" to get those types of blessings, and at that time, I wasn't. Now that I am older, I realize that was not at all true.

Often, we have questions and think they are too dumb, stupid, or crazy to ask. NEWS FLASH... The lack of understanding and wisdom keeps us stagnant and prevents growth.

My mindset on God's healing power changed in 1998, when my mother had a massive heart attack. Her heart stopped beating for several minutes. While watching the paramedics carry her body down the stairs administering CPR and giving her oxygen, my heart sank.Upon arrival at the emergency room, I was unable to see her. I was afraid. I did not know what to do; all I could do was pray. Once in the intensive care unit, I spoke with the physicians, and they told me that if my mother lived past the night, she would possibly be comatose. We were just unsure of what to do.

We prayed and read God's Word while we waited for God to perform a miracle - not only for her physical body to be healed, but also so that she would show no evidence of brain trauma. God did heal my mother and continues to heal her over and over again.

The Power of Forgiveness

Healing can be achieved in various ways; one way is to forgive. For many of us, we have been married to unforgiveness for a long time.

According to Merriam-Webster, unforgiveness is defined as *the unwillingness or the inability to forgive*. I'd like to further add that unforgiveness is the inability to let go of emotions or feelings of pain or hurt caused by someone or something.

Unforgiveness only hurts you when you hold on to it. Anger hardens your heart, causes health issues, and creates stress, which can lead to death.

Unforgiveness gives person who hurt you control over you. Healing for some may happen immediately, but for me, it has been a journey.

Likewise, you must be willing to forgive yourself. This means making an intentional decision to release feelings of discontent, bitterness, anger, and hate. You must free yourself from the control of those who have harmed you. You can only control yourself. Trying to control others is a form of manipulation.

We must invest in and take an active role in our healing. God can speak the Word, but we are the ones who have to take action. Discipline is necessary to achieve this growth. Also, know that it is okay to be a little selfish in this area because God wants you to be free.

If you have to pull away from others to focus on yourself, that is okay too. Do not be afraid to launch out and receive what God has for you.

Always remember not to self-sabotage. Although the journey can be painful at times, do not give up and abort the process. You can do this! You can forgive others and yourself.

The Prophecy

Several years ago, I attended a very intimate worship service; it was unlike none I had attended before. The worship was unrestricted and unrestrained. When I walked through the doors, I immediately felt God's presence. The sound of worship filled the atmosphere, and the aroma of God's love filled the room.

I received a prophetic Word from God that night. The Word of the Lord to me was that God would heal my heart from so many shattered and broken pieces. I was also told that God would go back and heal my unconscious mind, my subconscious, and my conscious mind. I was unsure of what that truly meant at the time, but I accepted God's Word of healing.

In 2019, I was given the commission with several confirmations to write this book. I wanted to be obedient to God, so I started to write. It was not until I got to this chapter that I began to fully understand the prophetic word that I received years earlier.

The exercise that I went through back in Chapter Two in discovering my little girl involved God allowing me in my conscious mind to revisit my unconscious mind, so I could deal with the pain and hurt that I had experienced. This allowed both my subconscious and conscious minds to be healed.

I believe that healing is an ongoing journey. God wants to shift your mind and transform your thoughts. This means changing the way you think, and how you process your thoughts. It is choosing to think positively no matter what it may look or sound like.

Proverbs 4:23 (NIV) says, *Above all else, guard your heart and mind, for everything you do flows from it.*

Proverbs 18:21(AMP) admonishes us to be careful of the words we speak because *death and life are in the power of the tongue and those who love it and indulge it will eat its fruit and bear the consequences of their words.* **So, speak life over yourself, instead of death.** YOUR WORDS CREATE YOUR WORLD!

I Corinthians 13:11 (NIV) says, *When I became a man (woman), I put the ways of childhood behind me.* **I'd like to present to you this thought: when the child is healed the adult becomes present.**

For those of you who may be reading this book, I would like to offer you this prayer of healing.

Father God, My Abba.

I come before Your presence with thanksgiving in my heart. Father, I ask that You forgive me of my sins and teach me how to forgive others. Heal my heart from all trauma, pain, and disappointments caused by others and myself. Heal my heart in the places and spaces that I am unable to verbalize – the ones often expressed in my silence and my tears.

Father, heal my mind from memories that taunt me, fears that paralyze me, and anxieties that propel me into the unknown. Lord, help me to control and eliminate the negative racing thoughts that plague my mind. Strengthen me as I transform my mind into new ways of thinking as I read Your Word. Knowing that everything is possible as I trust You.

Now My Abba, wrap me in Your arms, embrace me with Your love, and cover me and protect me as I travel on my journey to healing and wholeness.

In Jesus' name. Amen.

God is still in the healing business. He can give you beauty for ashes and turn your mourning into dancing (Isaiah 61:3). He did it for me and He can do it for you too.

Reflection:

Are you ready to assume an active role in your healing? Write down the names of anyone you need to forgive, including yourself. What next steps do you need to take in your healing journey?

_____
_____
_____
_____
_____
_____
_____
_____
_____
_____
_____
_____
_____

The Word

Quick Scripture Reference Guide

Anger:

Psalm 14:29
Proverbs 15:1
James 1:19-20

Psalm 37:8
Proverbs 16:32
Ephesians 4: 26, 31-32

Confidence:

Joshua 1:9
Psalm 37:3

Isaiah 26:3
Philippians 1:6

Anxiety/Worry:

Deuteronomy 31:6
Psalm 86:7
I Peter 5:7

Matthew 6:25-34
Isaiah 41:10
Philippians 4:6-7

Depression:

Psalm 3:3
Psalm 42:5
Isaiah 41:10

Psalm 34:18
II Corinthians 7:6
Matthew 11:28

Faith:

Romans 10:17
Mark 11:23

Hebrews 11:1, 6
Romans 15:13

Fear:

Psalm 23:4
Psalm 27:1
Psalm 91:4-5
Psalm 34:4

Isaiah 41:10
II Timothy 1:7
Hebrews 13:5-6
I John 4:18

The Mind:

Proverbs 23:7
Philippians 4:8

Romans 12:2
II Corinthians 10:5

Forgiveness:

II Chronicles 30:9
Matthew 6:14
Psalm 103:12

Luke 6:37
I John 1:9-10
Mark 11:25

Trust:

II Samuel 22: 31-33
Psalm 31:14-15
Psalm 56:3-4

Psalm 62:8
Psalm 29:25
Hebrews 2:13

Loneliness:

Genesis 28:15
Isaiah 12:22
Psalm 25:16

Psalm 27:10 TLB
Psalm 46:10
John 14:18 TLB

Additional Scriptures:

Self-empowerment
Daily Affirmations

I LOVE ME.

I am loved.

I believe in me.

I am becoming whole.

I am enough.

I am an overcomer.

I have choices.

Healing begins when I participate in the process.

I choose faith over my fears.

I can do all things.

I am beautiful or handsome.

I have the ability to encourage myself.

I am powerful.

I have the power and the ability to take charge of my life one step at a time.

I am strong.

I am who God says I am.

I give myself permission to trust me.

I can choose the thoughts that I think.

I choose to forgive.

I have self-control and I can make the right decisions.

I choose to live every day in peace and love, not in confusion and chaos.

I choose to live and not die.

I am resilient.

I am amazing.

I am courageous.

I am unique.

I am thankful.

I am deserving.

I will live and not die.

I am not alone.

I have purpose.

I am proud of myself.

I embrace my flaws.

I am responsible.

When I fall, I will get up.

My mistakes make me stronger.

I am determined to succeed.

My goals are achievable.

Challenges make me stronger.

All of life's issues have a solution.

I will not give up.

I choose to close the doors to my past and open new doors to my future.

I am moving from good to greater.

Write your own affirmations.

Resources

Ask for Help!

There's nothing wrong with needing help! Therapy was a Godsend for my life. It was through therapy that I was able to unpack the trauma I had suppressed all those years and receive the healing I needed. The Word of God is powerful! Prayer does work! And I am in no way less a Christian because I went to therapy. There are times when we need a trained professional to help us walk through the pain, so we can receive our healing. It takes MATURITY and COURAGE to reach for help when needed.

If you are in a crisis and need help, speak to someone. There are national hotlines that can assist. Here are a few.

National Hotline For Mental Health Crises And Suicide Prevention
Text or Dial: 988
Hotline: 1-800-273-TALK (8255)
Available 24/7 via phone and online chat.

National Domestic Violence Hotline
Hotline: 1 (800) 799 – 7233
Available 24/7 via phone and online chat.

Rape, Abuse, and Incest National Network (RAINN) – National Sexual Assault Hotline
Hotline: 1 (800) 656-4673
Available 24/7 via phone and online chat.

Substance Abuse and Mental Health Services Administration (SAMHSA) Helpline
Hotline: 1 (800) 662 – 4357
Available 24/7 via phone and online chat.

ChildHelp National Child Abuse Hotline
Hotline: 1 (800) 422 – 4453
Available 24/7 via phone and text.

National Runaway Safeline
Hotline: 1 (800) 786 – 2929
Email: info@1800runaway.org
Available 24/7 via phone, email, forum, and online chat.

National Human Trafficking Hotline
Hotline: 1-888-373-7888
Text: 233733
Available 24/7 via phone and text.

The Author

Tonja Anderson Greene

ABOUT THE AUTHOR

Tonja Anderson Greene is a nurse, certified life coach, health and wellness advocate, and intercessor. She enjoys putting pen to paper to discover, extract, educate, convey, encourage, and maturate others to embrace life wholeheartedly and choose the path to healing and wholeness. She is inspired by God to share her personal journey to aide in healing matters of the heart.

CONTACT AUTHOR

Tonja Anderson Greene can be reached at *becausetheresmorepublishing.com/authors/*.

www.ingramcontent.com/pod-product-compliance
Lightning Source LLC
Chambersburg PA
CBHW070324100426
42743CB00011B/2550